STATES

MONTANA

A MyReportLinks.com Book

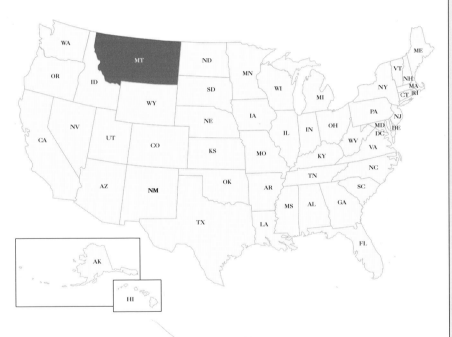

Judy Alter

MyReportLinks.com Books

an imprint of

 Enslow Publishers, Inc.

Box 398, 40 Industrial Road
Berkeley Heights, NJ 07922
USA

MyReportLinks.com Books, an imprint of Enslow Publishers, Inc. MyReportLinks is a trademark of Enslow Publishers, Inc.

Copyright © 2003 by Enslow Publishers, Inc.

All rights reserved.

No part of this book may be reproduced by any means without the written permission of the publisher.

Library of Congress Cataloging-in-Publication Data

Alter, Judy, 1938–
  Montana / Judy Alter.
    p. cm. — (States)
Summary: Discusses the land and climate, economy, government, and history of the Treasure State. Includes Internet links to Web sites related to Montana.
Includes bibliographical references and index.
  ISBN 0-7660-5136-6
  1. Montana—Juvenile literature. [1. Montana.] I. Title. II. Series:
States (Series : Berkeley Heights, N.J.)
F731.3.A45 2003
978.6—dc21

                              2002014855

Printed in the United States of America

10 9 8 7 6 5 4 3 2 1

To Our Readers:
Through the purchase of this book, you and your library gain access to the Report Links that specifically back up this book.
The Publisher will provide access to the Report Links that back up this book and will keep these Report Links up to date on **www.myreportlinks.com** for three years from the book's first publication date.
We have done our best to make sure all Internet addresses in this book were active and appropriate when we went to press. However, the author and the Publisher have no control over, and assume no liability for, the material available on those Internet sites or on other Web sites they may link to.
The usage of the MyReportLinks.com Books Web site is subject to the terms and conditions stated on the Usage Policy Statement on **www.myreportlinks.com**.
A password may be required to access the Report Links that back up this book. The password is found on the bottom of page 4 of this book.
Any comments or suggestions can be sent by e-mail to comments@myreportlinks.com or to the address on the back cover.

Photo Credits: © 1996 Montana Cyberzine, p. 25; © 1999 PhotoDisc, p. 18; © Corel Corporation, pp. 3, 10 (flag); © Donnie Sexton/Travel Montana, pp. 11, 13, 27, 40, 44; Big Horn County Museum, p. 34; C. M. Russell Museum, p. 14; DiscoveringMontana.com, p. 32; Enslow Publishers, Inc., pp. 1, 10, 19; Jeannette Rankin Foundation, p. 30; Library of Congress, p. 38; MyReportLinks.com Books, p. 4; PBS, *New Perspectives on the West*, p. 42; The Gary Cooper Estate/Seven Bar Nine, LLC, p. 16; The World Museum of Mining, p. 22; Travel Montana, pp. 20, 28, 37.

Cover Photo: © 1999 PhotoDisc.

Cover Description: Glacier National Park.

Contents

MyReportLinks.com Books
Great Books, Great Links, Great for Research!

MyReportLinks.com Books present the information you need to learn about your report subject. In addition, they show you where to go on the Internet for more information. The pre-evaluated Report Links that back up this book are kept up to date on **www.myreportlinks.com**. With the purchase of a MyReportLinks.com Books title, you and your library gain access to the Report Links that specifically back up that book. The Report Links save hours of research time and link to dozens—even hundreds—of Web sites, source documents, and photos related to your report topic.

Please see "To Our Readers" on the Copyright page for important information about this book, the MyReportLinks.com Books Web site, and the Report Links that back up this book.

Access:

The Publisher will provide access to the Report Links that back up this book and will try to keep these Report Links up to date on our Web site for three years from the book's first publication date. Please enter **SMT3997** if asked for a password.

Report Links

 The Internet sites described below can be accessed at
http://www.myreportlinks.com

*EDITOR'S CHOICE

▶ **World Almanac for Kids Online: Montana**
The *World Almanac for Kids Online* provides essential information
about Montana. Here you will find facts related to government,
population, economy, state symbols, and much more.

Link to this Internet site from http://www.myreportlinks.com

*EDITOR'S CHOICE

▶ **Montana Historical Society**
At the Montana Historical Society you can explore the museum's
collections and learn about Lewis and Clark's adventures in Montana.
You will also discover a "Student Guide to the History of the State."

Link to this Internet site from http://www.myreportlinks.com

*EDITOR'S CHOICE

▶ **Montana Kids**
Montana Kids Web site provides in-depth information about Montana's
agriculture and business, plants and animals, history, and an assortment
of topics related to the state. You will also find fun games.

Link to this Internet site from http://www.myreportlinks.com

*EDITOR'S CHOICE

▶ **Frontier House**
This PBS documentary attempts to answer the question of whether or
not a modern-day family could survive the frontier life. Here you will
learn about the experiences of three families who lived in frontier
houses in Montana.

Link to this Internet site from http://www.myreportlinks.com

*EDITOR'S CHOICE

▶ **Explore the States: Montana**
America's Story from America's Library, a Library of Congress Web site,
tells the story of Montana. Learn about local legacies, such as ax
throwing, cowboys, farmers, and the Battle of Little Bighorn.

Link to this Internet site from http://www.myreportlinks.com

*EDITOR'S CHOICE

▶ **Exploring with Lewis And Clark**
Follow the trail that Lewis and Clark followed during their expedition.
The interactive map reveals points of discovery as well as other points
of interest. You can also read journal entries and view a time line.

Link to this Internet site from http://www.myreportlinks.com

The Internet sites described below can be accessed at
http://www.myreportlinks.com

▶ **"Chief Joseph" Hin-mah-too-yah-lat-kekt (1840–1904)**
PBS's "New Perspectives on the West" Web site provides a brief overview
of Chief Joseph.

Link to this Internet site from http://www.myreportlinks.com

▶ **C. M. Russell Great Falls, Montana**
After his sixteenth birthday, C. M. Russell came to Montana's Judith Basin. Here
you will learn about Russell's life as an artist and his many other interests.

Link to this Internet site from http://www.myreportlinks.com

▶ **Discovering Montana**
Montana's official state Web site offers information about tourism and
recreation, doing business, government, education, and life in Montana.
You will also find links to the governor's Web site.

Link to this Internet site from http://www.myreportlinks.com

▶ **Fact Monster: Montana**
Fact Monster provides an overview of Montana. Here you will find a brief
introduction to Montana, facts and figures, geography, economy, government,
and history.

Link to this Internet site from http://www.myreportlinks.com

▶ **Gary Cooper**
Born in Helena, Montana, Gary Cooper became a symbol of the West. At the
official Gary Cooper Web site you can read his biography and view a list of
the many films he appeared in.

Link to this Internet site from http://www.myreportlinks.com

▶ **Glacier National Park**
The National Park Service Web site provides a brief overview of Glacier
National Park, located in northwest Montana. Click on "InDepth" to find
a history of the park and view photographs.

Link to this Internet site from http://www.myreportlinks.com

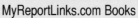

Report Links

The Internet sites described below can be accessed at
http://www.myreportlinks.com

▶**Jeannette Rankin Foundation**
Jeannette Pickering Rankin was the first woman elected to the United
States Congress. At the Jeannette Rankin Foundation Web site you will
find Rankin's biography, political memorabilia, photographs, and articles.

Link to this Internet site from http://www.myreportlinks.com

▶**Lewis & Clark**
Explore the adventures of Lewis and Clark through interactive stories,
living histories, and biographical information. You will also find time
lines, journals, and maps.

Link to this Internet site from http://www.myreportlinks.com

▶**Montana**
At this Web site you can explore things to do in Montana. You will also
find links to history, historical sites, and articles related to historical events.

Link to this Internet site from http://www.myreportlinks.com

▶**Montana: Big Sky Country**
This Web site provides a listing of links to facts and statistics about
Montana. You will also find an image of the state flag and links to
maps of Montana.

Link to this Internet site from http://www.myreportlinks.com

▶**Montana Cyberzine**
The Montana Cyberzine Web site contains articles about Montana and
its history, a travel guide, a points of interest page, and a search engine
designed to search all things Montana!

Link to this Internet site from http://www.myreportlinks.com

▶**Montana: Indian Nations**
The Montana Indian Nations Web site provides a brief description of
native tribes, such as Blackfeet, Crow, Flathead, Fort Peck, and others.
You will also find links to more information about the tribes.

Link to this Internet site from http://www.myreportlinks.com

Report Links

The Internet sites described below can be accessed at
http://www.myreportlinks.com

▶ Montana Maps
Perry-Castañeda Library at the University of Texas at Austin holds maps of Montana, including state and historical city maps, as well as maps of national parks, monuments, and historic sites.

Link to this Internet site from http://www.myreportlinks.com

▶ Montana's Missouri River Country
At Montana's Missouri River Country Web site you will learn about fishing on the Missouri River. You will also find information about dinosaurs, Lewis and Clark, history and culture, and hunting.

Link to this Internet site from http://www.myreportlinks.com

▶ Nez Perce National Historical Park
The National Park Service Web site provides a brief overview of Nez Perce Park, which is located in four states—Idaho, Montana, Oregon, and Washington.

Link to this Internet site from http://www.myreportlinks.com

▶ The Official Web Site Of Yellowstone National Park
Yellowstone National Park is located in Idaho, Montana, and Wyoming. At the official Yellowstone National Park Web site you can take an online tour of the park, explore its history, and plan a visit.

Link to this Internet site from http://www.myreportlinks.com

▶ The 100 Most Influential Montanans of the Century
At this Web site you will find descriptions of Montana's most influential people, including Gary Cooper, Ted Turner, Lee Metcalf, and many others.

Link to this Internet site from http://www.myreportlinks.com

▶ Stately Knowledge: Montana
The Stately Knowledge Web site provides a brief outline of facts about Montana. You will also find links to additional information about the state.

Link to this Internet site from http://www.myreportlinks.com

Report Links

> The Internet sites described below can be accessed at
> **http://www.myreportlinks.com**

▶ **Sun River Homestead**

The Homestead Act of 1862 encouraged many people to move west. This PBS documentary, "Sun River Homestead," explores several cities in Montana that people migrated to, including Helena, Sun River Valley, Spokane, Missoula, and Miles City.

Link to this Internet site from http://www.myreportlinks.com

▶ **Today In History: Custer's Last Stand**

Here you will learn about the day that General Custer found Sitting Bull by the Little Bighorn River in Montana and ordered an attack.

Link to this Internet site from http://www.myreportlinks.com

▶ **Today In History: Montana**

Today In History, a Library of Congress Web site, provides a brief history of Montana.

Link to this Internet site from http://www.myreportlinks.com

▶ **Travel the Bozeman Trail**

The Travel the Bozeman Trail Web site tells the history of this trail and provides a time line of events related to the trail. Diary entries of those who traveled the Bozeman Trail help you to experience the journey west.

Link to this Internet site from http://www.myreportlinks.com

▶ **U.S. Census Bureau: Montana**

The United States Census Bureau Web site provides essential statistics on Montana. Here you will find quick facts about people, business, and geography.

Link to this Internet site from http://www.myreportlinks.com

▶ **World Museum of Mining**

The World Museum of Mining in Butte, Montana, is dedicated to preserving the town's mining history. This Web site provides brief descriptions of what you will find at the museum and additional links to more information about Butte, Montana.

Link to this Internet site from http://www.myreportlinks.com

Montana Facts

Capital
Helena

Gained Statehood
November 8, 1889, the forty-first state.

Population
902,195*

Bird
Western meadowlark

Tree
Ponderosa pine

Flower
Bitterroot

Fossil
Duck-billed dinosaur

Mammal
Grizzly bear

Fish
Blackspotted cutthroat trout

Gemstones
Sapphire and agate

Song
"Montana" (lyrics by Charles Cohan and music by Joseph E. Howard)

Ballad
"Montana Melody" (words and music by Carleen and LeGrande Harvey)

Motto
Oro y plata ("Gold and silver")

Nicknames
Treasure State, Big Sky Country

Seal
A round seal illustrating the state's history and geography. At the top, a sunrise shines over snow-covered mountains. Three tools are in the center of the seal—a pick, a shovel, and a plow, symbols of the importance of farming and mining in Montana. Behind the tools are waterfalls, mountains, hills, trees, and cliffs.

Flag
State seal set on a blue rectangle with yellow edges. The word "Montana" is written in yellow across the top. The flag is modeled on one taken into battle during the Spanish-American War in 1898 by Montana volunteers.[1]

*Population reflects the 2000 census.

The Treasure State

The name "Montana" comes from the Spanish word *montaña*, meaning "mountainous." Most Americans think Montana was part of the old Wild West of the late nineteenth century. Montana had its share of hunters and trappers, battles between American Indians and white settlers, miners, sodbusters, cattlemen, and homesteaders. Actually, it was not quite as wild as the Western movies would have us believe. The state remained rural until well into the twentieth century; today, it has modern cities. It is home to major Strategic Air Command (SAC) air bases and missile sites, but much of Montana remains open.

▶ Historic Sites

Many of the most interesting sites to visit in the state relate to its history. The Little Bighorn Battlefield National Monument is fifty-four miles east of Billings. It marks the site of the battle between Sioux

Although scenes such as this ▶ one are common in Montana, the state has become more urban in the last century.

and Crow warriors and the U.S. Army's 7th Cavalry. That battle is often called Custer's Last Stand. Lieutenant Colonel George Armstrong Custer was a headstrong man who had been a Civil War hero. On June 25, 1876, he marched on an American Indian camp without waiting for back-up troops and without knowledge of the size of the camp. The 210 men of Custer's 7th Cavalry faced several thousand warriors, led by Crazy Horse, Sitting Bull, and other chiefs. Custer and all his men were slain.[1]

A visitors' center displays ancient artifacts and photographs. Stone monuments within an iron-rail fence mark the site of a mass grave of soldiers, scouts, civilians, and American Indians who were with Custer. Visitors walking that site today can feel the awesome burden of history.

The Custer Battlefield is within the Crow Nation reservation. The Little Bighorn Casino is nearby. Each year in August, the largest American Indian rodeo in the country is held there. Over five thousand tipis are erected on the grounds.

Virginia City is one of the world's most faithfully preserved placer (or surface) mining towns. It attracts 250,000 tourists a year and boasts historic structures from the 1860s. The stone barn that served as an opera house now hosts the Virginia City Players. Visitors may dine in the old Wells Fargo Building. A reconstructed blacksmith's shop houses original blacksmithing tools. The city's newspaper, *The Madisonian*, is the oldest weekly newspaper in the nation. It has been in operation since November 1871.[2]

Butte is home to the World History of Mining Museum. In Butte, tourists may see remnants of another classic mining town. Mining there went far below the surface. Long-deserted slag heaps (piles of garbage left behind after mining), mine shafts and equipment, mill yards, and the mansions of the wealthy mine owners still remain. There is a bit of "Chicago meets the Wild West" atmosphere to downtown. The city is also noted for its annual St. Patrick's Day celebration.[3] Indeed, many Montanans are descendants of Irish immigrant miners.

Pompey's Pillar, near Billings, is a huge sandstone rock with American Indian petroglyphs (etchings) and pictographs (paintings) of animals and flowers on its walls. It is named in honor of the infant son of Sacajawea.[4] This young Shoshone woman traveled with Lewis and Clark on their expedition in the early nineteenth century. She offered the explorers help with American Indian words and helped them find suitable food. Her presence in the group was something of a peace symbol to the American Indians they encountered.

A religious sect known as Hutterites has colonies in central Montana. Hutterities are called an Anabaptist

▲ Pompey's Pillar, located 30 miles outside of Billings, rises 200 feet above the Yellowstone River. On July 25, 1806, William Clark carved his name and the date into the large sandstone rock.

Welcome to Adobe GoLive 4 - Microsoft Internet Explorer

File Edit View Favorites Tools Help

Address http://www.cmrussell.org/nav2.html

C.M. Russell Museum
Great Falls, Montana

VISITOR GUIDE
MEET C.M. RUSSELL
LOG STUDIO & RUSSELL HOME
EVENTS & EXHIBITIONS
OTHER ARTISTS
MUSEUM SHOP
MEMBERSHIP
EDUCATION & TOURS

"Signal Smoke," C.M. Russell, oil, 24" x 36"

Done, but with errors on page.   Internet

C. M. Russell came to the Judith Basin shortly after his sixteenth birthday to live the life of a cowboy. Montana and its culture strongly influenced both his art and philosophy.

religion because they oppose infant baptism. They fled persecution in Europe as early as the seventeenth century. Today, they live on farming communes. Two-story houses, neat picket fences, sheds, and outbuildings are typical of their settlements. The Hutterites wear plain homemade clothing in keeping with their simple lifestyle. However, they do use modern farm machinery and drive pickup trucks and other vehicles.

Near Great Falls, visitors can see Ulm Pishkun. Early American Indians hunted buffalo by driving them over a cliff—a pishkun, or buffalo jump. Others would wait below to slaughter the stunned and injured animals. In the 1940s and 1950s, the bone pile at the base of Ulm Pishkun was plundered for use as fertilizer.[5]

Famous Montanans

Western artist Charles M. Russell (1864–1926) was probably Montana's most famous citizen. He was a successful, self-taught painter and a talented sculptor. Russell left his St. Louis home at sixteen for Montana and the American West that fascinated him. Action paintings of cowboys roping a grizzly or riding a horse into a saloon as a prank are typical Russell topics. Today, Russell's Great Falls home and the studio behind it are open to the public.

Montana can claim a number of authors as long-time residents. Dorothy M. Johnson (1905–84), who grew up in the state, worked as an editor in New York for many years. In the 1950s, she returned to Montana and to western subjects. Some of her short stories—*The Hanging Tree, A Man Called Horse,* and *The Man Who Shot Liberty Valance*—were made into movies.

A. B. Guthrie, Jr., (1901–91) is best known for six novels that chronicle Montana history from frontier times to the mid-twentieth century. His *The Big Sky* (1947) is about fur trappers. Spike Van Cleve, a cowboy, wrote about his life in *Forty Years' Gatherin's* (1977). His book fits into the bunkhouse tradition of storytelling, which was named for loggers who would sit in a circle in a bunkhouse and tell stories to pass the time. Norman Maclean (1902–90) left Montana to teach English at the University of Chicago. His *A River Runs Through It and Other Stories* (1976) is a classic work about his home state and about fly-fishing. It, too, was made into a movie. Contemporary writer Ivan Doig is perhaps best known for his autobiographical *This House of Sky* (1978).

G A R Y C O O P E R . C O M
The Official Gary Cooper Website

High Noon (1952)

Movie Poster

Movie Poster

Lobby Card
(Mexican Release)

back   next

▲ *Born Frank James Cooper in Helena, Montana, Gary Cooper served as an icon for the American male. The popular actor appeared in ninety-two films throughout his lifetime, often playing the role of a cowboy or adventurer.*

Wallace McRae of Forsyth is one of the American West's best-known cowboy poets.

Other famous Montanans include movie actor Gary Cooper, famous for his role as the reluctant sheriff in the classic *High Noon*. Actress Myrna Loy, star of *The Thin Man* (1934), and television newscaster Chet Huntley grew up in Montana. In 1916, Jeannette Rankin (1880–1973) was the first woman elected to the U.S. House of Representatives. A pacifist, she was one of the few to vote against the United States' involvement in World War I and World War II.

Land and Climate

Montana has three distinct geographic regions: western, central, and eastern Montana. Western Montana lies west of the Continental Divide and on top of the Rocky Mountains. Rivers to the east of the Divide flow toward the Gulf of Mexico and the Atlantic Ocean. Rivers to the west flow toward the Pacific.

The Western region begins at Glacier National Park and extends south to the city of Anaconda. Its eastern boundary is the Bob Marshall Wilderness in Flathead National Forest. The Bitterroot Mountains form the western border between Idaho and Western Montana. Missoula, with a population of 57,053 in 2000, is the largest city in this part of the state.[1] Wood products, retail trade, and tourism are the basis of its economy. The University of Montana is in Missoula.

Central Montana extends east from the Continental Divide. It is a region of broad valleys and occasional mountain ranges. Canada forms the northern border, and the Beartooth Mountain Range and Yellowstone National Park make up the southern border. The beginnings of the Yellowstone and Missouri rivers lie within this part of the state. In the nineteenth century, beaver, mink, and otter were plentiful here. Today, residents raise sheep, cattle, hay, and grains. Great Falls, with a population of 56,690 in 2000, is the largest city in this region.[2]

Eastern Montana is "Big Sky Country." It is vast ranch and farmland country bordered by Canada to the north, North Dakota and South Dakota to the east, and

▲ *Glacier National Park covers more than one million acres of northwestern Montana. Its rich ecological structure is the home to over 70 species of mammals and over 260 species of birds.*

Wyoming to the south. Within its boundaries are badlands (barren areas with many rocks), such as the Missouri Breaks and Makoshika State Park. The wetlands of the Yellowstone, Bighorn, and Missouri rivers are here. Billings, with a population of 89,847 in 2000, is the largest city in the state.[3] Oil and gas refining, transportation, trade, and the processing of agricultural products drive its economy.

Montana is the fourth-largest state in the United States with a land area of 145,552 square miles. At its widest east to west, it measures 550 miles; at its farthest north to south, 320 miles.[4]

A Varying Climate

Montana's geographic location and its diverse terrain contribute to its varied climate. Weather can be extreme and unpredictable. Lows can fall below −35°F, and highs can top 100°F. The lowest temperature ever recorded in the state was −70°F at Rogers Pass in January 1954. This is a record low temperature for the United States, excluding Alaska. The highest recorded temperature in Montana was 117°F at Glendive in 1893 and again in Medicine Lake in July 1937. Montana has the largest range in temperature of any state. Spells of bitter cold in the winter are often broken by warm, dry Chinook winds from the west.[5] The growing season is thirty-nine days in the high mountains and valleys. In the Yellowstone River basin, it is 150 days.[6]

Rainfall and humidity levels for Montana are low. West of the Divide, the average precipitation—rain and

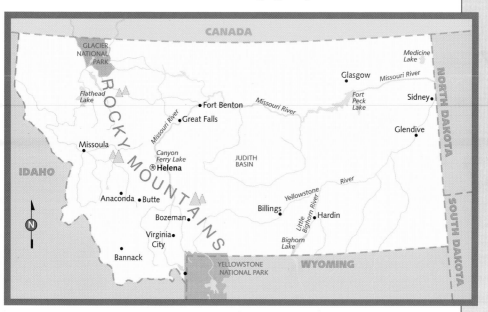

A map of Montana.

melted snow—is just under twenty inches. In the east, precipitation averages thirteen inches. The wettest months in the mountains are December and January. For the plains and valleys, May and June are the wettest.[7]

▷ An Environmental Enlightenment

In the past, Montanans, like many Americans, have misused the land. They did not realize nature's supplies could run out. Hunters and trappers killed off beaver, mink, and otter. Farmers plowed up the land without caring for it. Miners cut great gashes and holes in the earth. Today, Montanans are using what they have learned from the past to evaluate land use in the twenty-first century. They must safeguard Montana's natural resources for future generations, while pursuing economic development.

◁ Montana's snow-capped mountains allow for winter activities such as downhill and cross-country skiing and snowmobiling.

Chapter 3

Economy

Historically, Montana's economy has been based on three activities: cattle raising, mining, and agriculture. The state's climate, distance from major markets, and natural resources have shaped its economic development.

▶ A Dominant Industry

Cattle came before mining. Nineteenth-century Montana was the ideal land for cattle. It had rich grasses—blue grama, buffalo grass, and western wheatgrass. The first real cattle trade began in the 1850s on the Oregon Trail. Cattlemen sold beef to westward-bound settlers. Gradually local markets developed, especially in mining towns as those hastily-built communities grew. With the decline of mining in the 1870s, the local cattle markets failed. Cattlemen had to drive their herds long distances to railheads.

Cattle raising boomed again in the 1880s. By then, the bison, or buffalo, were gone. Many had been killed by hide hunters and diseases caught from domestic cattle. The destruction of the northern buffalo herd left the range open for grazing cattle. Investors from all parts of the country and even foreign countries established large cattle-raising operations in Montana. Local ranchers, who raised shorthorns, were particularly displeased when herds of Texas longhorns arrived.

Granville Stuart was one of the state's most famous cattle raisers. He began his career in Montana as a miner. He soon learned that there was more profit in selling

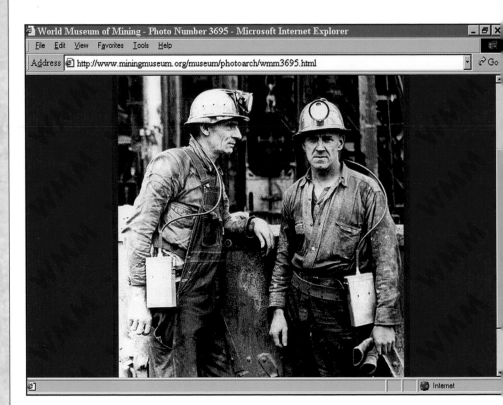

World Museum of Mining - Photo Number 3695 - Microsoft Internet Explorer

File   Edit   View   Favorites   Tools   Help

Address 🔁 http://www.miningmuseum.org/museum/photoarch/wmm3695.html   🔁 Go

Internet

▲ *Mining has played a large role in Montana's history.*

cattle to other miners. By the 1880s, he was grazing five thousand head of cattle at the foot of the Judith Mountains. Stuart gladly welcomed the Northern Pacific trains to the territory in 1883. Railroads made a huge impact on the cattle industry. Transportation of cattle by rail made the long cattle drives unnecessary.

▷ Cattle Dilemmas and Solutions

Along with diseases, cattle faced serious threats from wolves and coyotes, prairie fires, and rustlers. In 1885, ranchers formed the Montana Stockgrowers Association, mostly to deal with rustlers, or cattle thieves. Many cattle-men became vigilantes (people who take the law into their own hands). In the spring of 1884, they killed at least fifteen suspected rustlers, mostly by hanging.[1]

The winter of 1886–87 was disastrous for cattlemen. A spell of severe cold, wind, and snow struck. The temperature fell to −63°F. Ice covered the ground, and cattle could not get to the little grass there was. About 362,000 cattle starved or froze to death.[2] The "Big Die-Up," as it is sometimes called, led to the end of the open range. Ranchers began to fence their pastures. Charles Russell's painting *The Last of 5,000* shows a wolf watching a dying steer.

The novel *The Virginian*, by Owen Wister, tells the story of open-range ranching. *The Virginian* gave America its idea of the cowboy-hero. The real cowboy was dirty, dusty, dull, and could not shoot a gun. He worked for thirty dollars a month and "found," which basically meant food and shelter.

Welcome to the Treasure State

Montana has rich deposits of silver, copper, and other minerals. While gold is not central to mining in Montana, there was a gold rush in the late 1850s and early 1860s. Towns such as Bannack swelled in population as men tried their hand at placer mining (washing gold out of surface gravel). Most were disappointed, but eventually the area around Helena generated $30 million.[3] After the gold played out, miners dug for silver.

Mining towns were not as wild as the movies would have people believe. It is true, though, that they did not attract families. They did, however, attract gamblers and bartenders. Men outnumbered women. There were many minorities, including a large number of African Americans. The Chinese Americans were the largest minority and the most frequent target of acts of racism.

Miners did not get rich, and their life was hard. They did not have regular meals, clean clothes, or comfortable living quarters.

Crime was high in the camps, from gambling to claim jumping (the taking of another's claim, or land settlement) to murder. The court system did not always punish criminals. As they had done with cattle rustlers, Montana's citizens took the law into their own hands. Vigilantes operated in the mining camps. They hanged twenty-four men in a two-month period in 1864. Their victims included Henry Plummer, sheriff of Bannack, who supposedly led a gang of thieves.

▶ The Copper Industry

Copper eventually became more important than silver and gold. In 1884, the Anaconda Reduction Works made Montana the leading copper-producing state. Marcus Daly, a Montanan, owned the company. He bought up adjoining mines, built a copper reduction works and a smelter, and established a town named Anaconda. In 1895, Standard Oil bought out Anaconda. Control of the company then passed out of local hands.

Although people still called it Anaconda, the Anaconda Copper Mining Company became the Amalgamated Copper Company. The company dominated the economic, social, and political life of Montana for much of the twentieth century. Students of Montana government spoke openly of "a politics of copper."[4] By the 1970s, the company also produced and sold brass, cable, and wire. It was an international company, controlling one fourth of the world's copper.

In the 1970s, Atlantic Richfield bought the company. Shortly afterward, the Chilean government seized Anaconda mines in that country. This caused great financial

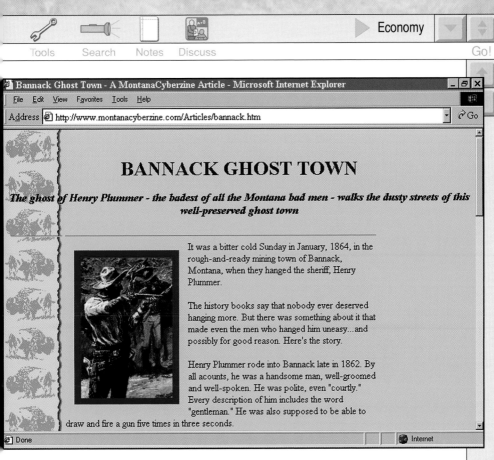

BANNACK GHOST TOWN

The ghost of Henry Plummer - the badest of all the Montana bad men - walks the dusty streets of this well-preserved ghost town

It was a bitter cold Sunday in January, 1864, in the rough-and-ready mining town of Bannack, Montana, when they hanged the sheriff, Henry Plummer.

The history books say that nobody ever deserved hanging more. But there was something about it that made even the men who hanged him uneasy...and possibly for good reason. Here's the story.

Henry Plummer rode into Bannack late in 1862. By all acounts, he was a handsome man, well-groomed and well-spoken. He was polite, even "courtly." Every description of him includes the word "gentleman." He was also supposed to be able to draw and fire a gun five times in three seconds.

▲ *Great controversy surrounds Henry Plummer, a sheriff of Bannack, who was hanged for being a member of "the Innocents," a murderous gang. Some claim he was the head of the Innocents while others say he was in no way a part of the ruthless mob. To this day many say his ghost walks the streets of Bannack, crying out for justice.*

losses to the company. The Montana branch of Anaconda closed its operations in Butte and laid off many employees. Other smaller companies, using higher technology, moved into Montana. Today, copper mining is important to the state's economy, but it no longer dominates.[5]

▶ Farmers' Struggle

Montana has two main agricultural products: wheat and beef. Generally, they are produced in large ranching and farming operations. These provide 86 percent of the products the state sends to national and international markets.

The state's spring and winter high-protein wheat is in demand throughout the world.

Some agricultural activity first developed to supply mining towns. Yet, farmers did not come to the Montana plains in great numbers until after 1900. New land policies, land promotions, and improved farming methods and machinery made it possible to farm the dry but flat eastern part of the state. Between 1900 and 1923, settlers filed 114,620 homestead claims on 25 million acres of land.[6]

Dreams of reclaiming the moisture in the land with water from rivers were impractical. Federal irrigation attempts failed. Most farming was dryland, using patterns of tilling the soil that conserved the water already in it. In alternate years, farmers let land lie fallow (unplanted). They plowed deep and left loose topsoil to hold down evaporation.

Farmers had a hard life. Cattle ranchers looked down on them. The very first immigrant farmers lived in sod houses or tar-paper shacks. Homes made from rip-sawed boards later replaced both. Farmers had social lives within their communities. At threshing, or harvest time, they helped each other. Prosperity came in cycles marked by periods of drought and depression.

Today, some small farms struggle to grow sugar beets, corn, hay, and barley. These farms are disappearing, though, as young people move to the city. This trend is not unique to Montana. Throughout the world, young people are leaving rural areas for more urban places in search of higher-paying jobs.

▶ A Popular Vacation Spot

Lumber, coal, and oil have grown in importance in the state. However, the only real growth industry has been tourism. The creation of Yellowstone National Park in 1872 and Glacier National Park in 1910 established Montana as a tourist site. Then, the railroad and the automobile revolutionized tourism. Both made access to these now world-famous sites faster and easier. Today, tourism brings millions of dollars to the state and employs thousands of workers.

Effects of a Shifting Economy

Montana trails most other states in economic development. It has not attracted high-tech industries and has lost high-paying jobs—many in the mining industry. In 1988, the income per person in the state was 22 percent below the national average. This is a dramatic decline from 1950. At that time, Montanans' per capita income was 8 percent above the national average.[7]

In 1910, President Taft established the nation's tenth national park, Glacier National Park. Twenty-two years later, the U.S. and Canadian government combined Glacier National Park with Waterton Lakes National Park, located just across the border in Canada, to make Waterton-Glacier International Peace Park. This lasting symbol of peace and friendship between the two countries is the first ever created. The parks were named a World Heritage Site in 1995, because both are Biosphere Reserves.

Chapter 4

Government

Montana became a territory of the United States in 1864. The territorial government passed laws restricting women and foreigners, particularly the Chinese. There were also obvious religious and racial prejudices. The state remained a territory for twenty-five years. A constitutional convention in 1866 tried for statehood but failed. In 1884, voters ratified the constitution of a second convention, although it was not approved by Congress. The fault was less with Montana than with the power struggle in Washington, D.C., between the two major parties. Republicans blocked the admission of Montana, which, at that time, was heavily Democratic. In 1889, the United States

◀ *Excavation for Montana's capitol building, located in Helena, began in 1875. Setbacks kept the building from being completed until 1902.*

government promised immediate statehood if Montana submitted an acceptable constitution. The third constitutional convention took place in July 1889. This constitution limited the power of the executive branch and gave equal representation to rural counties. The state's population voted in favor of the constitution. They cared little for the details—they wanted statehood.[1] Montana became the forty-first state on November 8, 1889.

Overcoming Political Division: Senator Mike Mansfield

Montana has traditionally sent Democrats to Washington, D.C., and elected Republicans to state offices. The race between the two parties was always extremely competitive and sometimes unpleasant. Ranchers and owners of large farms tend to be conservative and belong to the Republican Party. They gather support from various corporations. Laborers, owners of small farms, lawyers, university faculty, and students generally are liberal and support the Democratic Party. They are supported by labor unions. In the 1980s, the liberals and labor unions lost power, as they did throughout the West.

Montanans like their politicians to be down-home friendly. Senator Mike Mansfield was one of the best known. Most people in Montana called him simply "Mike." First elected to the U.S. House of Representatives in 1942, he served for ten years. Following his tenure in the House, he served as a U.S. senator from Montana until 1977. A liberal Democrat, he was the Senate majority leader longer than anyone else in American history. After retiring from the Senate, Mansfield became the U.S. ambassador to Japan. He held this post until 1988.

▶ A Progressive State

Over the years, amendments and elections modified the original constitution. In 1914, Montana gave women the right to vote—five years before the Nineteenth Amendment made women's suffrage national. One reform streamlined government by reorganizing state agencies. Another gave voters the power to reject, amend, or create taxes. In 1969, a commission was appointed to study the state constitution. It had not been amended since its

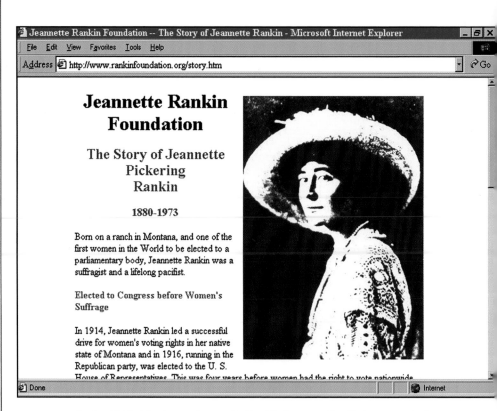

Jeannette Rankin Foundation -- The Story of Jeannette Rankin - Microsoft Internet Explorer

File   Edit   View   Favorites   Tools   Help

Address http://www.rankinfoundation.org/story.htm   Go

Jeannette Rankin Foundation

The Story of Jeannette Pickering Rankin

1880-1973

Born on a ranch in Montana, and one of the first women in the World to be elected to a parliamentary body, Jeannette Rankin was a suffragist and a lifelong pacifist.

Elected to Congress before Women's Suffrage

In 1914, Jeannette Rankin led a successful drive for women's voting rights in her native state of Montana and in 1916, running in the Republican party, was elected to the U. S. House of Representatives. This was four years before women had the right to vote nationwide

Done   Internet

△ *In 1916, Montanan Jeannette Rankin became the first woman to be elected to the U.S. Congress. As a two-term member of the U.S. House of Representatives, she fought for women's rights, including the vote, and for peace. A statue of Congresswoman Rankin stands at the Statuary Hall of the U.S. Capitol Building, placed there by the State of Montana in 1985.*

ratification in 1889. A new, progressive constitution was adopted in 1972.[2]

Montana's Legislature

The Montana legislature consists of a senate and a house of representatives. There are fifty senators elected to a four-year term and one hundred representatives elected to a two-year term from the state's one hundred legislative districts. Candidates must be eighteen years of age, residents of Montana for one year, and residents of their district for six months. Montana has fifty-six counties. A county with low population shares a legislative district with another county. A five-member Districting and Apportionment Committee can decide the number of districts for equal representation. Reapportionment follows the U.S. Census every ten years.

The first territorial capital was Virginia City. In 1874, the capital was moved to Helena. The legislature meets there in odd-numbered years at noon on the first Monday in January. They meet for ninety days, and the meetings are open to the public. Any Montana citizen may testify before the legislature or contact a representative. Legislative sessions are occasionally extended. The legislature may also be called into special session when necessary.

Everyone Has a Voice

Any Montana citizen eighteen years or older has a right to lobby professionally. An individual must apply for a license from the Commissioner of Political Practices and pay a fee of fifty dollars. Montana regards lobbyists as a source of important information.[3] The most influential lobby groups represent cattlemen and miners.

Taxation is a major issue in Montana. The state has both property taxes and income taxes. In 1993, voters rejected a general sales tax for the second time in twenty-two years.[4] Only 3 percent of the American population does not pay sales tax.[5]

The Executive Branch

The executive branch of the government consists of the governor, lieutenant governor, secretary of state, attorney general, auditor, superintendent of public instruction, and five public service commissioners. These leaders are elected for four-year terms in November of even-numbered years. They take office the following January. Elected

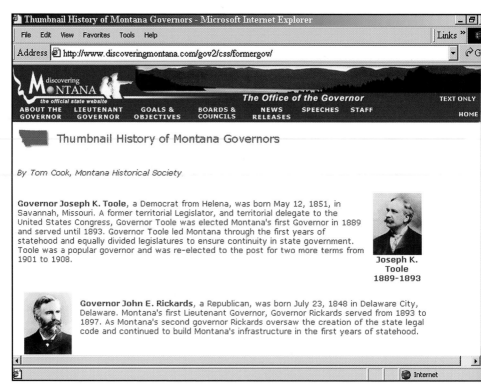

△ Joseph K. Toole was the first governor of the state of Montana. A Democrat from Helena, he served three terms as the state's chief executive.

officials must keep public records of the activities of their office.

Judicial Review

Montana has a three-level court system, with the state supreme court at the top. There are twenty-one district courts with thirty-seven judges. They try civil cases and felony criminal cases. The third level, courts of limited jurisdiction, includes justice of the peace courts. They try misdemeanor cases. Also at this level are city and municipal courts, which deal with city ordinances. Finally, there are special courts to deal with workers' compensation issues and water rights issues.

Local Government

In 2000, Montana had 128 incorporated cities and towns in fifty-six counties, many with low population.[6] County governments handle tax collection, record keeping (births, marriages, and deaths), roads and bridges, county fairs, and extension services. A board of county commissioners, which may meet as often as every day, governs each county.

Montana has nine federally-recognized tribal governments. On each reservation, the tribal government regulates domestic relations; levies taxes; controls conduct; holds elections; develops health and educational programs; manages the tribal economy and natural resources; and maintains relations with local, state, and federal governments. Tribal governments determine who is legally a member of the tribe. They also grant hunting and fishing licenses for their land. They have jurisdiction over tribal members but not over nontribal individuals who commit crimes on reservation property. After negotiating with the state, tribes may operate casino games and dog and horse races.[7]

History

About eight thousand years ago, the American Indians who occupied present-day Montana were hunters and gatherers. They hunted the mammoth, an ancestor of the bison, or buffalo. Two thousand years ago, natives were nomadic, moving from place to place to hunt bison. The bison supplied many of their needs for clothing, shelter,

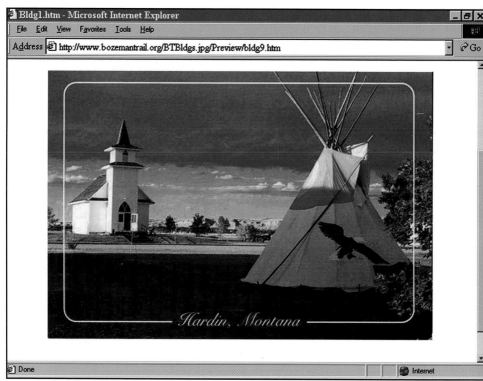

Bldg1.htm - Microsoft Internet Explorer

File   Edit   View   Favorites   Tools   Help

Address http://www.bozemantrail.org/BTBldgs.jpg/Preview/bldg9.htm   Go

Done   Internet

▲ Structures that have been preserved at the Big Horn County Museum, just outside Hardin, Montana, give visitors a glimpse into Montana's past.

tools, food, and fuel. They also gathered wild turnips, wild onions, and a wide variety of berries and herbs.

Present-day American Indian tribes probably arrived in the 1600s and 1700s. They include the Flathead, Kutenai, Pend d'Oreille, Shoshone, Gros Ventre, and Nez Percé. In the 1700s, Spanish explorers brought the horse to the Plains Indian tribes. This changed their lives dramatically. They could now hunt more efficiently and move their villages more easily. By the 1800s, the major American Indian tribes in the area were the Arapaho, Blackfeet, Crow, Flathead, Kutenai, Pend d'Oreille, Salish, Shoshone, and Sioux (Lakota, Dakota, and Nakota).[1]

Lewis and Clark

Meriwether Lewis and William Clark were the first known white explorers to cross present-day Montana. Today, they are heroes in the state. President Thomas Jefferson commissioned Captain Lewis and Lieutenant Clark to explore the Northwest Territory. Today, most people refer to their Corps of Discovery as the Lewis and Clark Expedition. The Corps left St. Louis in the spring of 1804 and reached present-day Montana in late April 1805. Sacagawea, their Shoshone guide and translator, helped them trade for horses with her tribe. After reaching the Columbia River and the Pacific Ocean, they returned through Montana in 1806.

Lewis and Clark provided valuable information about the American Northwest. They mapped the land, recorded facts about wildlife and plants, and established friendly relations with the Indian tribes they met.

The Fur Trade

Fur traders from Britain and France may have entered Montana before Lewis and Clark. However, the fur trade

really developed after their expedition. Fur traders were real pathfinders. They knew every hole, corner, and stream in the American West. Trappers hunted mostly beaver, which was in great demand for high-fashion hats popular in the East. Famous trappers, or mountain men, include Jim Bridger, Jedediah Smith, and William Sublette.

Along with guns and alcohol, the traders introduced pots, pans, dye, beads, knives, and ribbon to the American Indians. Smallpox and other diseases not previously known to American Indians were horrific by-products of trade with whites in those early years. The fur trade also destroyed the ecological balance of the area by almost eliminating certain groups of animals. Indeed, only a small number of people, who lived far from Montana, profited from the fur trade. By the late 1830s, the fur trade had fallen apart. Beaver were scarce, and beaver hats were no longer fashionable in New York.

Through their contact with fur traders, some Flat-head Indians converted to Roman Catholicism. A delegation from the tribe walked all the way to St. Louis to ask Jesuit priests to come to Montana. Father Pierre Jean DeSmet established St. Mary's Mission in the Bitterroot Valley in 1841. Priests brought European medicine and surgery to the American Indian Tribes in Montana.[2]

▶ Dreams of Gold

The fur trade may have come first, but gold brought many more adventurers to Montana. Montana's gold rush came in the mid-1800s. In 1863, ten thousand people came to Alder Gulch. The mining camp later became Virginia City.[3] In the 1860s, Montana was the second largest gold-producing state in the United States.[4]

Montana became the second largest gold-producing state in the nation during the 1860s.

The discovery of gold made Fort Benton on the Missouri River a major port. Mining equipment arrived there by steamboat. Then the equipment was transported to mining towns over the newly-created roads. Freighting companies and stage lines flourished.

The "Indian Problem"

Wagon trains that were headed to Montana's gold fields left the Oregon Trail for a shortcut—the Bozeman Trail, named after John Bozeman. This trail crossed American Indian hunting grounds. Led by Oglala Sioux chief Red Cloud, the Sioux attacked many travelers along this trail. In December 1866, Captain William J. Fetterman took eighty-one soldiers to protect a wagon train. The entire troop was killed. Red Cloud's War (1866–67), as the conflict was called, forced the government to negotiate. Under the terms of the 1868 Treaty of Fort Laramie, the Bozeman Trail and Forts Reno, Phil Kearny, and C. F. Smith were closed.

The Montana Territory was one of the last areas of the United States where Indian nations held large areas of land. In the late 1800s, newly-arriving white settlers, or pioneers, wanted this land for mining, farming, and ranching. Due to settlers' demands for land, the government kept squeezing the American Indian peoples into smaller sections of land.

Some American Indians reacted by raiding, stealing livestock, begging for food and whiskey, and occasionally killing settlers. The military acted in haste and, more often than not, killed innocent Indians rather than those who had done the raiding.

▷ The Battle of Little Bighorn (1876)

The most famous battle between Montana's settlers and the American Indians really began outside the territory. Gold was discovered in the Black Hills of the Dakotas. This was sacred land for the Sioux Nation. In fact, the entire territory was part of the Great Sioux Reservation. This reservation had been set up under the terms of the 1868 Treaty of Fort Laramie. According to the treaty, the United States government agreed to keep white settlers out of the territory.

◁ *Lieutenant Colonel George Armstrong Custer's fate was sealed at the Little Bighorn.*

Then, Lieutenant Colonel Custer led an expedition that opened this land to miners. Sioux Indian chiefs Sitting Bull and Crazy Horse refused to stop younger braves from raiding the miners' camps. The Indian Bureau called in the army. A major campaign against the Sioux and their Northern Cheyenne allies was planned. Leading one of the attacking forces, Custer planned to surprise the American Indians who had camped along the Little Bighorn River in southern Montana. The Cheyenne, Sioux, and Arapaho warriors there, however, outnumbered Custer and his men four to one, and his entire regiment was killed. The date was June 25, 1876. It was the last victory for the Indians in America.

Indian Reservations

Chief Joseph led a band of Nez Percé that chose not to move onto the reservation in Oregon in 1863. Then, in 1877, the band (about one third of the Nez Percé) was required to move onto the reservation. Chief Joseph was willing. However, some young warriors angrily killed some whites. Fearing retaliation, most of the Nez Percé with Chief Joseph tried to cross Montana and find safety from punishment in Canada. The army pursued them. Within miles of the border, the hungry and exhausted American Indians surrendered. In a speech, Chief Joseph said, "From where the sun now stands, I will fight no more."[5]

With the surrenders of Chief Joseph and Crazy Horse in 1877 and Sitting Bull's death in 1890, many American Indians had little choice but to move to reservations. Settling on reservations meant survival. In reality, reservation life was difficult. There were never enough rations for the Indians. By the 1890s, however, the "Indian problem" was considered solved.

▲ *The Little Bighorn Battlefield National Monument contains the Custer National Cemetery. This is where more than five thousand unidentified bodies were buried in a common ground. Headstones have been placed on the battlefield where it is thought each soldier fell.*

▶ Growing Prosperity

At the turn of the century, Montana's population grew dramatically. Most newcomers settled on the eastern plains. In 1909, the federal government amended the Homestead Law of 1862, giving settlers better terms. A head of a household or anyone over twenty-one could claim 320 acres of land. The law required a house—or shack—be built on the property and the land cultivated for gain. Many single women even took up claims. By 1920, the state's population was almost 500,000.[6]

In the early 1920s, prosperity seemed on the way in spite of a drought that struck in 1917. New industries moved into the state. Major oil fields in Montana increased petroleum production, and metal prices rose. Montana became a dude ranch state—one in which some ranches operate as resorts, whose guests, or dudes, dress in western garb, including cowboy hats and boots. Guests typically enjoy horseback riding and other sports as well as campfire cookouts. The dude ranches brought "city folks" (and their money) to Montana. Few people were unemployed.

Not all was law and order. About six hundred residents of Montana were members of the Ku Klux Klan. Bootleggers—individuals who make, transport, or sell goods illegally—seemed to flourish. In fact, Butte, Montana, led the nation in the drinking of illegal whiskey during Prohibition.[7] The Eighteenth Amendment to the U.S. Constitution prohibited (forbid) the manufacture and sale of alcoholic beverages in the United States. Prohibition was repealed in 1933.

Falling on Hard Times

The drought continued. By the mid-1920s, half of Montana's farmers had lost their land. They could not pay the mortgage. Banks failed because their loans went unpaid. Montana was the only state in the nation to lose population between 1920 and 1930.[8]

Montana's hard times worsened with the Great Depression of the 1930s. President Franklin D. Roosevelt's New Deal brought some relief to Montana residents. The New Deal was Roosevelt's plan for bringing the United States out of the Depression. Montana received $1 million from the Federal Emergency Relief Administration and the Civil Works Administration.[9] One agency of the New Deal, the Civilian Conservation Corps (CCC), carried out a reforestation

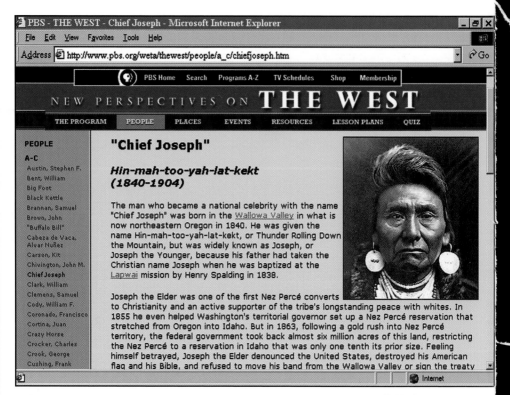

PBS - THE WEST - Chief Joseph - Microsoft Internet Explorer

File Edit View Favorites Tools Help

Address http://www.pbs.org/weta/thewest/people/a_c/chiefjoseph.htm   Go

PBS Home   Search   Programs A-Z   TV Schedules   Shop   Membership

NEW PERSPECTIVES ON **THE WEST**

THE PROGRAM   PEOPLE   PLACES   EVENTS   RESOURCES   LESSON PLANS   QUIZ

PEOPLE
A-C
Austin, Stephen F.
Bent, William
Big Foot
Black Kettle
Brannan, Samuel
Brown, John
"Buffalo Bill"
Cabeza de Vaca,
Alvar Nuñez
Carson, Kit
Chivington, John M.
Chief Joseph
Clark, William
Clemens, Samuel
Cody, William F.
Coronado, Francisco
Cortina, Juan
Crazy Horse
Crocker, Charles
Crook, George
Cushing, Frank

"Chief Joseph"

Hin-mah-too-yah-lat-kekt
(1840-1904)

The man who became a national celebrity with the name "Chief Joseph" was born in the Wallowa Valley in what is now northeastern Oregon in 1840. He was given the name Hin-mah-too-yah-lat-kekt, or Thunder Rolling Down the Mountain, but was widely known as Joseph, or Joseph the Younger, because his father had taken the Christian name Joseph when he was baptized at the Lapwai mission by Henry Spalding in 1838.

Joseph the Elder was one of the first Nez Percé converts to Christianity and an active supporter of the tribe's longstanding peace with whites. In 1855 he even helped Washington's territorial governor set up a Nez Percé reservation that stretched from Oregon into Idaho. But in 1863, following a gold rush into Nez Percé territory, the federal government took back almost six million acres of this land, restricting the Nez Percé to a reservation in Idaho that was only one tenth its prior size. Feeling himself betrayed, Joseph the Elder denounced the United States, destroyed his American flag and his Bible, and refused to move his band from the Wallowa Valley or sign the treaty

Internet

Chief Joseph is remembered for his fight against the injustices of the United States government in their dealings with the American Indians.

program that had forty camps and employed 25,600 men.[10] Through this program, forest areas that had been cleared were replanted. Other federally-funded projects in the state included improved roads, bridges, new school buildings, and new or improved water mains.

Resurgence of the Economy

Prosperity seemed to return to Montana with World War II. The drought was over. The demand for copper, lumber, oil, and gas increased. Mining flourished. The agriculture industry bounced back as the federal government became its greatest consumer.

There were difficulties as well during the war. Tourism fell. Gas and tires were rationed. Men and women left the state to enlist in the armed services and to find defense jobs. Over 1,500 citizens of Montana were killed or missing in action.[11]

Post-World War II

After the war, Montana's population increased again. Defense projects were located in Montana, including much of the underground nuclear force. An Army Air Force base was established at Glasgow, and Malmstrom Air Force Base was enlarged. The economy still did not grow dramatically. Few new industries developed, and population growth was slow.

By 1960, Montana had more citizens living in urban and suburban settings than rural ones. Even so, it had only 4.7 people per square mile. This was less than one tenth of the national average. The federal government was still the largest landholder in the state.[12]

The federal Wilderness Act of 1964 raised people's awareness of the value and beauty of America's landscape. Montana began to conserve its national resources. Montanans had learned firsthand the lasting and harmful effects of waste and pollution. The constitution adopted in 1972 declared "a clean and healthful environment" an inalienable right. In the late 1980s and 1990s, tourism became Montana's fastest-growing industry. Robert Redford's film, *A River Runs Through It* (1993), caused a swell in tourism and people moving to Montana.[13]

Still Holding On to the Past

Today, Montana faces two directions. It looks toward the Pacific Northwest with which it has strong economic ties.

By land, water, and banking, it is joined to the Great Plains, Chicago, and to Minnesota, where markets for grain and beef are important.

Montana, perhaps more than other western states, looks inward. Residents cling to its nineteenth- and early twentieth-century heritage. Lewis and Clark, cattleman Granville Stuart, and artist Charles M. Russell are heroes. Montana citizens identify with the pioneer spirit. They believe in the value of unspoiled space and the survival of the toughest.[14] Space and distance still dominate in the state. It is certainly not a coincidence that agriculture, including raising cattle, and tourism produce the greatest income for a state nicknamed "Big Sky Country."

▲ Custer National Forest, covering 1.2 million acres of land, is one example of how Montanans value natural beauty. The most ecologically-diverse forest in the northern region, this forest provides a habitat for grizzly bears, elk, deer, mountain goats, and many other animals.

Chapter Notes

Montana Facts

1. John B. Wright, *Montana Places: Exploring the Big Sky Country* (Mesilla, N.Mex.: New Mexico Geological Society, 2000), pp. 3–4; www.montanakids.com.

Chapter 1. The Treasure State

1. John Whiteclay Chambers, ed. *The Oxford Companion to American Military History* (New York: Oxford Press, 1999), p. 397.

2. John B. Wright, *Montana Places: Exploring the Big Sky Country* (Mesilla, N.Mex.: New Mexico Geological Society, 2000), p. 44.

3. Nicko Goncharoff, *Rocky Mountains*, 2nd ed. (Melbourne: Lonely Planet Publications, 1999), p. 680.

4. Wright, p. 9.

5. Ibid., pp. 5–6.

Chapter 2. Land and Climate

1. *Time Almanac 2003* (Boston.: Family Education Network, Inc., 2002), p. 158.

2. Ibid.

3. Ibid.

4. Ibid.

5. John B. Wright, *Montana Places: Exploring the Big Sky Country* (Mesilla, N.Mex.: New Mexico Geological Society, 2000), p. 3.

6. Andrea Merrill and Judy Jacobson, *Montana Almanac* (Helena, Mont.: Falcon Publishing, Inc., 1997), p. 42.

7. Ibid., p. 38.

Chapter 3. Economy

1. Michael P. Malone, Richard B. Roeder, and William L. Long, *Montana: A History of Two Centuries* (Seattle: University of Washington Press, 1991), p. 183.

2. Ibid., p. 166.

3. Clark C. Spence, *Montana: A Bicentennial History* (New York: W. W. Norton & Company, Inc.), p. 20.

4. Ibid., p. 177

5. Malone, Roeder, and Long, pp. 323–324.

6. Ibid., p. 232.

7. Ibid., p. 346.

Chapter 4. Government

1. Michael P. Malone, Richard B. Roeder, and William L. Long, *Montana: A History of Two Centuries* (Seattle: University of Washington Press, 1991), pp. 194–198.

2. Ibid., pp. 195–198.

3. Andrea Merrill and Judy Jacobson, *Montana Almanac* (Helena, Mont.: Falcon Publishing, Inc., 1997), p. 189.

4. Ibid., p. 217.

5. Malone, Roeder, and Long, p. 387.

6. Merrill and Jacobson, p. 199.

7. Ibid., p. 202.

Chapter 5. History

1. John B. Wright, *Montana Places: Exploring the Big Sky Country* (Mesilla, N.Mex.: New Mexico Geological Society, 2000), p. 3.

2. Andrea Merrill and Judy Jacobson, *Montana Almanac* (Helena, Mont.: Falcon Publishing, Inc., 1997), p. 106.

3. Michael P. Malone, Richard B. Roeder, and William L. Long, *Montana: A History of Two Centuries* (Seattle: University of Washington Press, 1991), p. 65.

4. Ibid., p. 68.

5. John Whiteclay Chambers, ed., *The Oxford Companion to American Military History* (Oxford: Oxford University Press, 1999), p. 535.

6. Merrill and Jacobson, pp. 116–117.

7. Clark C. Spence, *Montana: A Bicentennial History* (New York: W. W. Norton & Company, Inc.), p. 144.

8. Malone, Roeder, and Long, p. 283.

9. Ibid., p. 149.

10. Merrill and Jacobson, p. 118.

11. Spence, p. 162.

12. Ibid., p. 178.

13. Ibid., pp. 190, 193.

14. "Montana Timeline," *Montana Historical Society*, n.d., <http://www.Montanahistoricalsociety.org/departments/education/> (February 11, 2003).

Further Reading

Aylesworth, Thomas G. and Virginia L. *The Great Plains: Montana, Nebraska, North Dakota, South Dakota, Wyoming.* Broomall, Pa.: Chelsea House Publishers, 1995.

Bennett, Clayton. *Montana.* Tarrytown, N.Y.: Marshall Cavendish Corporation, 2001.

Capstone Press Geography Department, Patricia K. Kummer. *Montana.* Minnetonka, Minn.: Bridgestone Books, 2002.

Ferrell, Nancy Warren. *The Battle of the Little Bighorn in American History.* Springfield, N.J.: Enslow Publishers, Inc., 1996.

Koch, Elers, Peter Koch, and Jack Ward Thomas. *Elers Koch: Forty Years a Forester.* Missoula, Mont.: Mountain Press Publishing, 1999.

Ladoux, Rita, and Joyce Johnston. *Montana.* Minneapolis: Lerner Publications, 2002.

Shirley, Gayle C. *More Than Petticoats: Remarkable Montana Women.* Helena, Mont.: Falcon Publishing, Inc., 1995.

———. *Charlie's Trail: The Life and Art of C. M. Russell.* Helena, Mont.: Falcon Publishing, Inc., 1996.

Thompson, Kathleen. *Montana.* Austin, Tex.: Raintree/Steck-Vaughn, 1996.

Williams, Judith M. *Montana.* Danbury, Conn.: Children's Press, 2002.

Index